Common Core Lessons & Activities:
Key Events of World War I

By Carole Marsh
Published by Gallopade International, Inc.

Printed in the U.S.A. (Peachtree City, Georgia)

TABLE OF CONTENTS

G: Includes Graphic Organizer
GO: Graphic Organizer is also available 8½" x 11" online
download at www.gallopade.com/client/go
(numbers above correspond to the graphic organizer numbers online)

Causes of World War I

Use online or classroom resources to complete the graphic organizer. Describe the four key causes of World War I.

Nationalism	Imperialism

World War I

Militarism	Alliances

READING INFORMATIONAL TEXT

Archduke Franz Ferdinand

Read the text and answer the questions.

In 1878, Austria-Hungary took over Bosnia, a small country between Austria-Hungary and Serbia. Many Bosnians and Serbians were unhappy with Austria-Hungary's control of Bosnia.

In the early 1900s, Archduke Franz Ferdinand was next in line to become king of Austria-Hungary. He decided to visit Sarajevo, the capital of Bosnia. A group of Bosnian nationalists, with the help of Serbia, planned to assassinate the Archduke on his trip.

On June 28, 1914, the Archduke and his wife Sophie arrived in Sarajevo. They traveled to different events in a security convoy. The Bosnian nationalists tried to bomb Ferdinand's car, but were not successful. They did not give up. Later in the day, the convoy took a wrong turn down a side street. Bosnian nationalist Gavrilo Princip was standing on the street as Ferdinand and Sophie passed in their convertible. He shot and killed them both.

The Archduke's assassination prompted Austria-Hungary to declare war on Serbia for aiding the Bosnian nationalists. Within weeks, several countries, including Germany and Great Britain, were involved in the growing conflict.

1. A. Use a dictionary to define nationalist as it is used in the text.
   B. Why would a nationalist be angry with the government of Austria-Hungary?
2. A. Use a dictionary to define convoy as it is used in the text.
   B. Why did Ferdinand and Sophie travel in a convoy?
3. Explain why many Serbians were unhappy with Austria-Hungary's control over Bosnia. Use evidence from the text to support your answer.
4. What does it mean to "declare war"? Why did Austria-Hungary declare war on Serbia? Explain.
5. Research this event and list several reasons why Germany and Great Britain became involved in the conflict.

GRAPHIC ORGANIZER

Leaders of World War I

Use a classroom or online resource to complete the organizer. Describe each person's role in WWI and list their alliance: Allied or Central Powers.

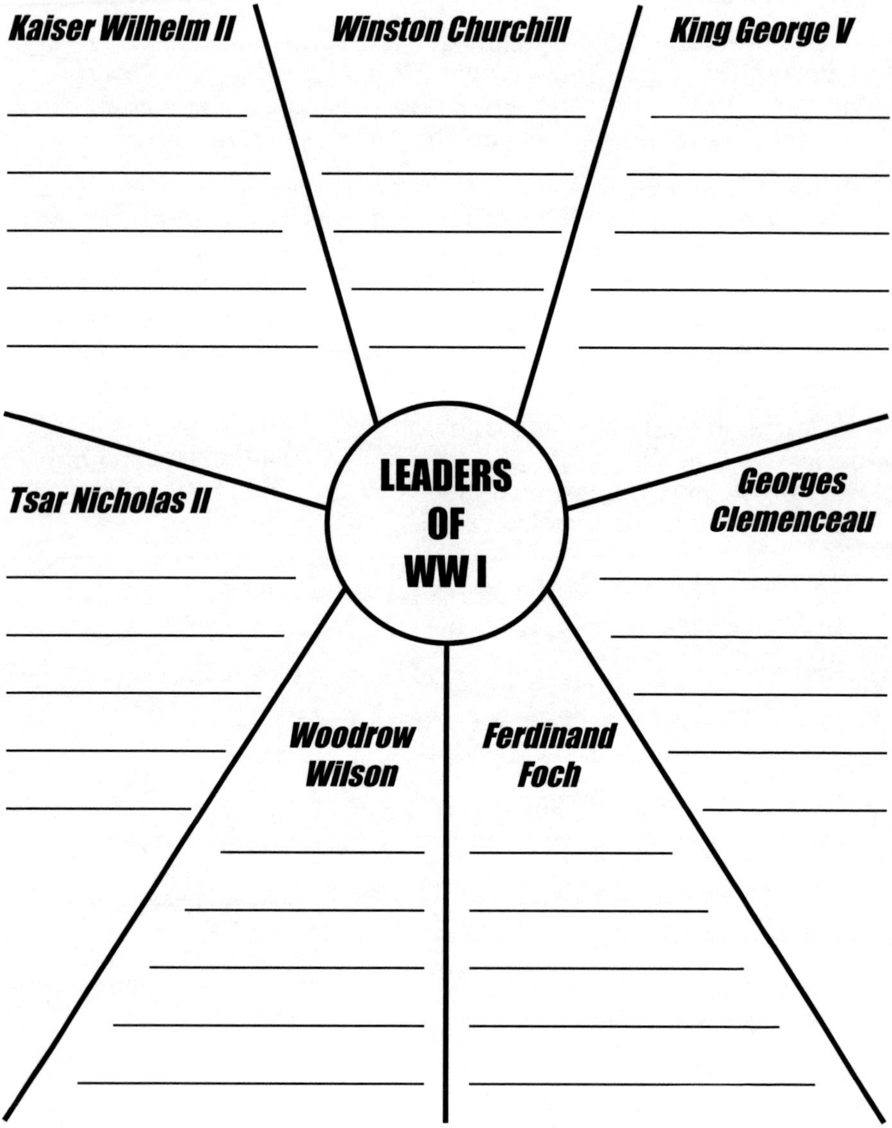

MAP ACTIVITY

Allied and Central Powers

Analyze the map and answer the questions.

1916 European Military Alliances

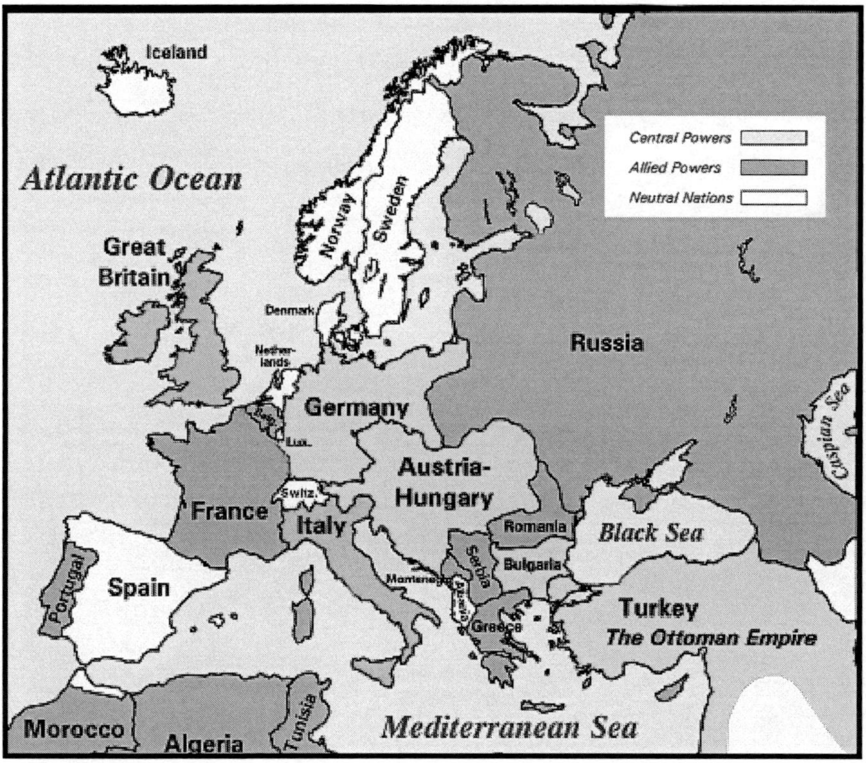

1. A. Use the map key to find the Allied and Central Powers.
   B. Make a list of Allied Powers, Central Powers, and neutral countries.
2. Using the map, explain how geography affects country alliances. What other factors might affect country alliances?
3. Explain why naval warfare was an important part of WWI.
4. The Allied Powers take up more space on the map. Do you think the size of a country helps win a war? In what ways can size be an advantage? In what ways can size be a disadvantage?

World War I Vocabulary

Use a dictionary and other resources to complete the graphic organizer for each vocabulary word.

armistice

doughboys

dreadnought

League of Nations

No Man's Land

Red Baron

Tommy

U-boats

blockade

duckboards

kaiser

Lusitania

propaganda

reparations

Treaty of Versailles

DEFINITION	FACTS/CHARACTERISTICS
WORD	
EXAMPLES	NON-EXAMPLES

Sinking of the *Lusitania*

This illustration depicts the sinking of the British ocean liner Lusitania by a German U-boat on May 7, 1915. More than 1,100 passengers died, including 128 Americans.

Look at the illustration and answer the questions.

Courtesy of The Illustrated London News

1. What do you notice first? Make 3-5 other observations.
2. Who do you think was the audience for this image? Why do you think the image was created?
3. What inferences can you make about the people in the small boats in the foreground? Explain.
4. What can you conclude about how the *Lusitania* sank? What details in the picture support your conclusion?
5. Describe how this illustration may have affected American opinions of WWI.
6. Write a short narrative from the perspective of a person on one of the lifeboats. Describe what you see, hear, smell, and feel. Present your work to the class.

READING INFORMATIONAL TEXT

Trench Warfare

Read the text and answer the questions.

Much of the fighting during WWI took place in trenches. Trenches were shallow, open-air tunnels dug into the ground. Allied and Central Powers soldiers dug trenches that stretched across thousands of miles of countryside.

The Allies used four main types of trenches. The front line trench sat only about a mile from the enemy line. Behind the front line trench, the support trench held soldiers and supplies to support the front line. The reserve trench sat behind the support trench and held more supplies and soldiers for emergencies. Communication trenches connected each trench for easy travel and communication. Between the Allied and enemy trenches was a strip of land called "No Man's Land" filled with barbed wire, craters, and artillery shells.

Thousands of soldiers died in the trenches. Close proximity to enemy fire made trench warfare very dangerous. Most attacks happened just before sunrise and just after sunset. During the day, no one could cross "No Man's Land" without being gunned down by the enemy. Along with dangerous combat, soldiers suffered through terrible living conditions. The trenches were dirty, rat-infested, and open to all the elements. Rain often flooded the trenches, making it almost impossible to sleep or stay warm.

Soldiers rotated their time in each trench to keep up morale. On average, soldiers spent one week at a time in the front line trench, then rotated to the support and reserve trenches. Trench warfare often lasted for months with only a few miles of ground gained in some places.

1. Use a dictionary to define morale as it is used in the text. How do you think rotation helped boost the soldiers' morale?
2. Based on the text, why do you think most trench attacks happened just before sunrise or just after sunset?
3. Explain why the land between trenches was called "No Man's Land."
4. Do you think trench warfare was effective? Why or why not? Use evidence from the text to support your answer.

PRIMARY SOURCE ANALYSIS

Life in the Trenches

Soldiers feared trench diseases almost as much as enemy fire. Diseases ranged from Trench Fever, a painful infection caused by lice dung, to Trench Foot, a bacterial infection that sometimes ended in amputation. Soldiers slept very little and often had to sleep on the ground in the middle of the day. Life in the trenches was very difficult.

Study the photograph below and answer the questions.

Courtesy of Wikipedia

1. What is the first thing you notice about this photograph? Make 3-5 additional observations.

2. What can you infer about the living conditions of WWI trench soldiers from this photograph?

3. Do you think these soldiers were in the front line, support, or reserve trench? What evidence from the photograph supports your answer?

4. Write a letter home from the perspective of a soldier in this photograph. Describe life in the trenches to your family. Proofread and edit your work.

Zimmermann Telegram

Use online and classroom resources to complete the graphic organizer. Describe why Germany sent the Zimmermann Telegram and list the telegram's end results.

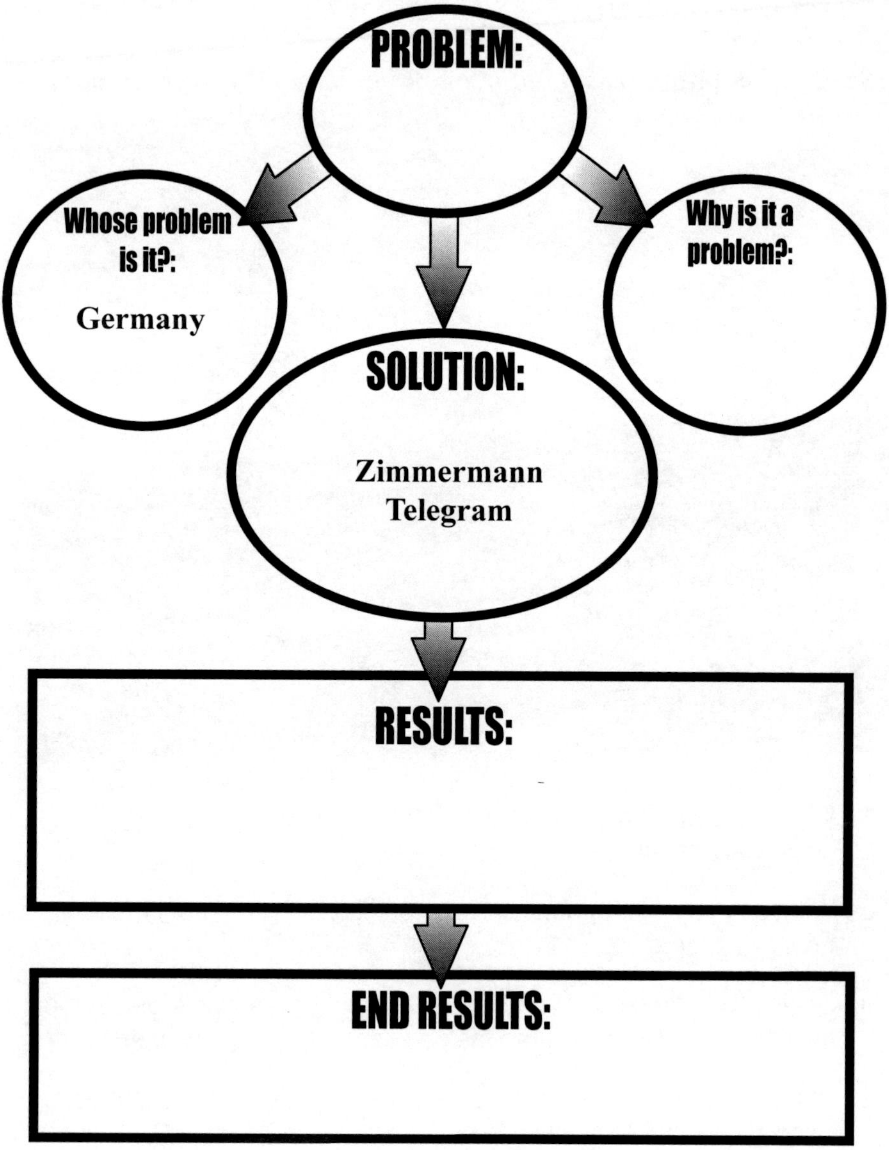

PRIMARY SOURCE ANALYSIS

I Want YOU for U.S. Army

Look at the poster and answer the questions.

Courtesy of the Library of Congress

1. Explain the purpose of the message at the bottom of the poster. Who is the intended audience?
2. Use a dictionary to define the word <u>recruit</u>. What was the purpose of adding “nearest recruiting station” to the poster?
3. Is this poster patriotic? List details from the poster to support your answer.
4. A. What tone does this poster portray?
   B. Does Uncle Sam’s expression and stance support the tone? Explain.
5. In your opinion, is this poster effective? Why or why not?

New Technologies in WWI

Complete the graphic organizer by describing each new technology and listing the effects it had on WWI.

Cause:
Machine Gun

Cause:
Zeppelin

Cause:
Tank

Cause:
Poison Gas

Cause:
Depth Charge

Cause:
Aircraft Carrier

Cause:
Anti-aircraft Gun

Cause:
Flamethrower

Effect:

Effect:

Effect:

Effect:

Effect:

Effect:

Effect:

Effect:

PRIMARY SOURCE ANALYSIS

Christmas Truce

On Christmas Day, 1914, soldiers fighting in the trenches on the Western Front called for an unofficial ceasefire. It began when German soldiers stepped out of their trenches unarmed with their hands up. At first, the Allied soldiers were afraid it was a trick. But soon, enemy soldiers met in No Man's Land and spent Christmas Day talking and sharing food and small gifts.

Read the quotations and answer the questions.

"A most extraordinary thing happened. . . . Some Germans came out and held up their hands and began to take in some of their wounded and so we ourselves immediately got out of our trenches and began bringing in our wounded also. The Germans then beckoned to us and a lot of us went over and talked to them and they helped us to bury our dead. This lasted the whole morning and I talked to several of them and I must say they seemed extraordinarily fine men. . . . It seemed too ironical for words."
– Lieutenant Geoffrey Heinekey

"I think I have seen one of the most extraordinary sights today that anyone has ever seen. About 10 o'clock this morning I was peeping over the parapet when I saw a German, waving his arms, and presently two of them got out of their trenches and some came towards ours. We were just going to fire on them when we saw they had no rifles so one of our men went out to meet them and in about two minutes the ground between the two lines of trenches was swarming with men and officers of both sides, shaking hands and wishing each other a happy Christmas."
– Second Lieutenant Dougan Chater, letter to his mother

1. Describe the tone of each quotation. Are they similar or different? Explain.
2. Explain the meaning of too ironical for words as it is used in the text.
3. Infer how the soldiers on both sides might have felt during the truce, and why. Cite evidence from the text to support your answer.
4. Write a letter home from the point of view of a German soldier on that day. Describe how you feel and what you see, hear, smell, and taste. Read your letter aloud to the class.

Important Battles of WWI

Read the description of these important battles of WWI and answer the questions.

Battle and Seige of Liege, August 1914 –This was the first battle on the Western Front. Belgian soldiers fought to hold back the Germans from advancing into the city of Liege. The Germans won the battle and took control of Liege.
Battle of the Frontiers, August 1914 – Several battles took place along the border of France and Germany and France and Belgium. The Germans steadily advanced toward Paris.
Race to the Sea, September-November 1914 – Over the course of several battles, Allied and German soldiers fought to reach the French and Belgium coasts first.
Battle of Verdun, February-December 1916 – This was the longest battle of WWI, lasting almost a year. French soldiers held off German troops from taking the city of Verdun.
Battle of Cambrai, November-December 1917 – This was the first use of tanks in a large battle. Allied armies staged a surprise attack with tanks against German armies.
Battle of Cantigny, May 1918 – This was the first attack by American armies on the Western Front. American soldiers captured the village of Cantigny and took 200 German prisoners.
Second Battle of Marne, July-August 1918 – This battle marked the turning point of the war. Allied soldiers pushed back German troops. This was the beginning of the retreat of German forces.

1. A. Divide into teams. Create a map of the battles listed above. Mark each location with a star and date. Present your maps to the class.
   B. What can you infer about the German army's goals from the location of each battle? What about the Allied army's goals?
2. Define the Western Front. Why was it a strategic battleground?
3. What inference can you make from the text about the success of America's involvement in WWI? Cite evidence from the text to support your answer.

Food Will Win the War

Look at the poster and answer the questions.

Courtesy of the National Archives

1. What is the first thing you notice about this poster? List 3-5 other observations.
2. Who is the intended audience of this poster?
3. In your own words, write a summary of each line of the poster. What is the purpose of the poster?
4. How does the illustration support the message of the poster? Cite evidence to support your answer.
5. In your opinion, is this poster effective? Why or why not? Discuss as a class.

Gas Mask

In WWI, poison gas was often used to injure soldiers in the trenches.

Study the photo and quotation, and answer the questions.

Courtesy of the Imperial War Museums

> "I wish those people who talk about going on with this war whatever it costs could see the soldiers suffering from mustard gas poisoning. Great mustard-coloured blisters, blind eyes, all sticky and stuck together, always fighting for breath, with voices a mere whisper, saying that their throats are closing..."
>
> – Vera Brittain, nurse
> *Testament of Youth: An Autobiographical Study of the Years 1900–1925*

1. Why did soldiers wear gas masks in WWI? Cite evidence from the primary sources in your answer.
2. What can you infer from the picture about how the soldiers felt in the gas masks? How do you think it affected their duties?
3. Write a journal entry from the perspective of a soldier during a gas attack. Describe your surroundings, the attack, the gas mask, and how you feel.
4. In your opinion, do you agree with chemical warfare? Why or why not? Discuss as a class.

Key Events of World War I

Put the events in chronological order in the graphic organizer. Discuss any cause/effect relationships as a class.

Sinking of the *Lusitania*	Second Battle of Marne	President Wilson presents his Fourteen Points	Assassination of Archduke Franz Ferdinand	Battle of Verdun
Germany signs armistice	United States declares war on Germany	Christmas Truce	The Treaty of Versailles	Battle of Liege

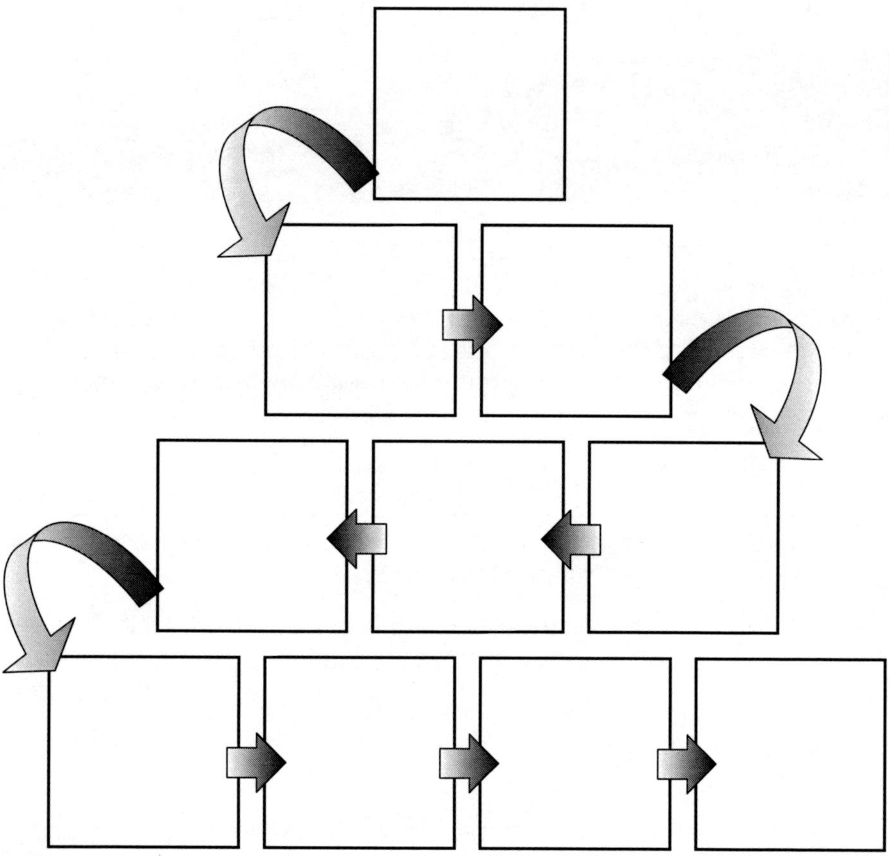

Fourteen Points

Read the text and answer the questions.

On January 8, 1918, President Woodrow Wilson presented his Fourteen Points speech in front of Congress. The speech described his goals to end WWI and laid out a plan for peace.

The points were divided into three main groups. The first five points addressed international concerns such as treaties, trade, and freedom of the seas. These points were included to help prevent future wars.

The next eight points described in detail boundary changes across Europe. Wilson believed groups should form their own nations based on ethnic identities. He hoped this would keep peace among different groups of people.

The fourteenth point was the creation of the League of Nations. The League was Wilson's idea to create a place where nations could gather and discuss complaints without resorting to war.

Wilson's Fourteen Points were distributed across America and Europe. While they respected his efforts for peace, the British and French were unhappy with Wilson's plan. They wanted stronger consequences for Germany and more protection from future wars. The "Big Four" nations, America, Britain, France, and Italy, made changes to the plan, including forcing Germany to pay reparations.

1. Create a computer presentation to present the Fourteen Points. Use online or classroom resources.
2. A. Use a dictionary and classroom resources to define ethnic identities as it is used in the text.
   B. Why did President Wilson believe nations should be formed based on ethnic identities?
3. What inferences from the text can you make about President Wilson's stance toward war and peace?
4. A. Use a dictionary to define reparations as it is used in the text.
   B. In your opinion, was it fair to have Germany pay reparations? Why or why not?

COMPARE AND CONTRAST

Europe During and After WWI

Analyze the maps and answer the questions.

Europe, 1915

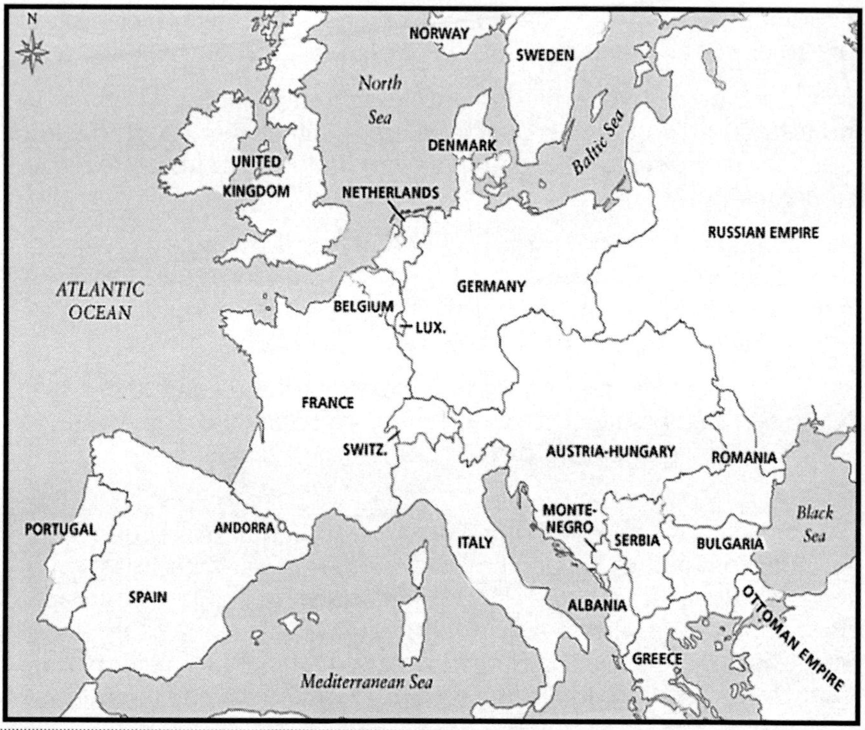

PART A: Use the maps to determine whether each statement is true or false.

1. ________ Austria-Hungary's borders did not change after WWI.
2. ________ Czechoslovakia was a new country created after WWI.
3. ________ Spain was split into two countries after WWI.
4. ________ Russia's border did not change after WWI.

PART B: Use the maps to identify what is being described.

5. These two countries were once called empires.
6. Hungary, Austria, and Czechoslovakia were once this country.
7. This country gained independence from Great Britain after WWI.

Europe, 1919

PART C: Make inferences from the maps to answer the questions.

8. What changes from 1915-1919 do you notice first? List 3-5 other observations.
9. What area of the map changed the most after WWI? Why?
10. How many countries existed in Europe during WWI? How many were there after WWI?
11. What changes were made to Russia after WWI? List every difference you see. Use evidence from the maps to support your answer.
12. Describe the transformation of Austria-Hungary after WWI. Why do you think this country changed so much? Explain.
13. Using President Wilson's Fourteen Points, what inferences can you make about why a few larger countries were split into several smaller countries?
14. Divide into teams. Using online and classroom resources, research the different ways a country's borders are formed. Using your research, what can you infer about how the United States' and your state's borders were formed?

Treaty of Versailles

Read the text and answer the questions.

Between January and June of 1919, the Allied Powers and Germany met in the Palace of Versailles in Paris to discuss a peace treaty. The goal for the treaty was to ensure peace and prevent future war. However, the Allied Powers, especially France, were still angry from the war, and Germany was not very involved in the peace talks. As a result, the nations signed the Treaty of Versailles, an agreement that forced strict requirements on Germany.

The Treaty was separated into 15 parts. Many of the parts dealt with Germany. Part I established the new League of Nations but did not allow Germany to become a member until 1926. Part II gave Germany new boundaries. Germany lost the land it had gained in the war as well as large portions of the country. Part III forced Germany to be demilitarized. Part IV took away all of Germany's colonies in other countries. Part V forced Germany's army to become very small and took away many of their large weapons. Part VIII forced Germany to pay billions of dollars in reparations and forced them to take responsibility for starting the war. Part IX forced Germany to pay for even more things.

While all the nations signed the treaty, Germany was not happy with the conditions. Some Americans were also unhappy with the strict requirements. They feared the tension between nations might affect Europe's economy and lead to another war.

1. A. Use a dictionary to define demilitarized as it is used in the text.
   B. Why was Germany forced to be demilitarized?
2. Why do you think France was angrier with Germany than other Allied Powers after the war? Explain.
3. What inferences can you make about how Germany's economy was affected by Part II and Part IV of the Treaty?
4. In your opinion, was the Treaty of Versailles a fair agreement? Cite evidence from the text to support your answer.
5. Predict Germany's response to the Treaty of Versailles. Cite evidence from the text to support your answer.

Effects of WWI on the United States

Complete the graphic organizer with the causes for each effect of WWI on the United States.

Cause:	→	Effect: America became a powerful industrial nation.
Cause:	→	Effect: America gave women the right to vote.
Cause:	→	Effect: African Americans moved to Northern cities.
Cause:	→	Effect: The U.S. experienced a deadly flu epidemic.
Cause:	→	Effect: Many Americans disliked getting involved in war.

Correlations to Common Core State Standards

For your convenience, correlations are listed page-by-page and for the entire book!

This book is correlated to the Common Core State Standards for English Language Arts grades 3-8, and to Common Core State Standards for Literacy in History, Science, & Technological Subjects grades 6-8.

Correlations are highlighted in gray.

PAGE #	READING *Includes:* RI: Reading Informational Text RH: Reading History	WRITING *Includes:* W: Writing WHST: Writing History, Science, & Technology	LANGUAGE *Includes:* L: Language LF: Language Foundational Skills	SPEAKING & LISTENING *Includes:* SL: Speaking & Listening
2	RI RH . 1 2 **3** 4 **5** 6 7 8 9 **10**	W WHST . 1 **2** 3 **4** 5 6 **7** 8 9 **10**	L LF . 1 2 3 4 5 6	SL . 1 2 3 4 5 6
3	RI RH . **1** 2 **3** **4** 5 6 7 **8** 9 **10**	W WHST . 1 **2** 3 **4** 5 6 7 **8** 9 **10**	L LF . 1 2 3 **4** **5** **6**	SL . 1 2 3 4 5 6
4	RI RH . 1 2 3 4 5 6 7 8 **9** **10**	W WHST . 1 2 3 4 5 **6** **7** **8** **9** **10**	L LF . 1 2 3 4 5 **6**	SL . 1 2 3 4 5 6
5	RI RH . 1 2 3 4 5 6 **7** 8 9 10	W WHST . 1 **2** 3 **4** 5 6 **7** 8 9 **10**	L LF . 1 2 3 4 5 6	SL . 1 2 3 4 5 6
6	RI RH . 1 2 3 **4** 5 6 7 8 9 **10**	W WHST . 1 2 3 4 5 6 7 8 9 10	L LF . 1 2 3 **4** 5 **6**	SL . 1 2 3 4 5 6
7	RI RH . **1** 2 **3** 4 **5** 6 **7** 8 9 **10**	W WHST . 1 **2** **3** **4** 5 6 7 **8** 9 **10**	L LF . 1 2 **3** 4 5 **6**	SL . 1 2 3 **4** 5 **6**
8	RI RH . **1** 2 **3** **4** **5** 6 7 8 9 **10**	W WHST . **1** **2** 3 **4** 5 6 7 8 9 **10**	L LF . 1 2 3 **4** 5 **6**	SL . 1 2 3 4 5 6
9	RI RH . **1** 2 **3** 4 5 6 **7** 8 9 10	W WHST . 1 **2** **3** **4** **5** 6 7 **8** 9 **10**	L LF . 1 2 **3** 4 5 **6**	SL . 1 2 3 4 5 6
10	RI RH . 1 2 **3** 4 **5** 6 7 8 9 **10**	W WHST . 1 2 3 4 5 6 **7** 8 **9** **10**	L LF . 1 2 3 4 5 6	SL . 1 2 3 4 5 6
11	RI RH . 1 **2** 3 4 5 6 **7** 8 9 **10**	W WHST . **1** **2** 3 **4** 5 6 7 8 9 **10**	L LF . 1 2 3 4 5 6	SL . 1 2 3 4 5 6
12-13	RI RH . 1 **2** 3 4 **5** 6 **7** 8 9 **10**	W WHST . 1 **2** 3 **4** 5 6 **7** 8 9 **10**	L LF . 1 2 3 4 5 6	SL . 1 2 3 4 5 6
14	RI RH . **1** 2 **3** **4** 5 **6** 7 8 **9** **10**	W WHST . 1 **2** **3** **4** 5 6 7 **8** **9** **10**	L LF . 1 2 **3** **4** **5** **6**	SL . 1 2 3 **4** 5 6
15	RI RH . **1** **2** 3 **4** 5 6 **7** 8 9 **10**	W WHST . 1 **2** 3 **4** 5 **6** 7 8 **9** **10**	L LF . 1 2 3 **4** 5 **6**	SL . 1 2 3 4 **5** 6
16	RI RH . **1** **2** 3 4 **5** 6 **7** **8** 9 **10**	W WHST . **1** **2** 3 **4** 5 6 7 8 **9** **10**	L LF . 1 2 **3** 4 **5** 6	SL . **1** **2** 3 4 5 6
17	RI RH . **1** **2** **3** 4 **5** 6 **7** 8 9 **10**	W WHST . **1** 2 **3** **4** 5 6 7 8 9 **10**	L LF . 1 2 3 4 5 6	SL . **1** 2 3 4 5 6
18	RI RH . 1 2 3 4 **5** 6 **7** 8 9 10	W WHST . 1 2 3 4 5 6 **7** 8 9 10	L LF . 1 2 3 4 5 6	SL . **1** 2 3 **4** 5 6
19	RI RH . **1** **2** **3** **4** **5** 6 7 **8** 9 **10**	W WHST . **1** **2** 3 **4** 5 **6** 7 8 9 **10**	L LF . 1 2 3 **4** 5 **6**	SL . 1 2 3 4 **5** 6
20-21	RI RH . **1** **2** **3** 4 **5** 6 **7** 8 **9** **10**	W WHST . 1 **2** 3 **4** 5 **6** **7** 8 9 **10**	L LF . 1 2 **3** 4 5 6	SL . **1** 2 3 4 5 6
22	RI RH . **1** **2** **3** **4** **5** 6 7 8 9 **10**	W WHST . **1** **2** 3 **4** 5 6 7 8 **9** **10**	L LF . 1 2 3 **4** 5 **6**	SL . 1 2 3 4 5 6
23	RI RH . 1 **2** 3 4 **5** 6 **7** 8 9 **10**	W WHST . 1 **2** 3 **4** 5 6 **7** 8 9 **10**	L LF . 1 2 3 4 5 6	SL . 1 2 3 4 5 6
COMPLETE BOOK	RI RH . **1** **2** **3** **4** **5** **6** **7** **8** **9** **10**	W WHST . **1** **2** **3** **4** **5** **6** **7** **8** **9** **10**	L LF . 1 2 **3** **4** **5** **6**	SL . **1** **2** 3 **4** **5** **6**

For the complete Common Core standard identifier, combine your grade + "." + letter code above + "." + number code above.

In addition to the correlations indicated here, the activities may be adapted or expanded to align to additional standards and to meet the diverse needs of your unique students!